SELF-DEFENSE KARATE

SELF-DEFENSE KARATE

SIHAK HENRY CHO

7th Dan Black Belt

STRAVON EDUCATIONAL PRESS · New York

CONTENTS

INTRODUCTION

During the past decade the United States has witnessed an unusually rapid increase in all types of crime. A frightening aspect of this trend is the rising number of physical assaults upon individuals. Every year police statistics and newspaper stories catalogue an increasing number of muggings, assaults, rapes, and attempted rapes. As a result, a knowledge of self-defense has become a necessity for both men and women.

Self-defense may be described as a series of coordinated movements that enable the individual to protect himself against attack. Effective self-defense requires a mastery of both defensive and offensive maneuvers. Too often it is not enough merely to evade the assailant's attack; rather one must be able to counterattack, rendering the assailant incapable of doing further harm.

Karate uses many parts of the body in both offensive and defensive ways. The punches, strikes, blocks, twists, and shifts of karate represent a variety of techniques that may be combined in offensive and defensive maneuvers. Some of the kicking techniques, virtually unknown in the United States, are quite easy to execute, making them especially effective self-defense procedures.

Combative sports such as boxing and wrestling do prepare the participants in forms of self-defense, but these sports require considerable strength and physical contact, and consequently are generally open only to men. Karate, however, requiring only a minimum of strength and physical contact, has become the favorite type of self-defense for women. Unlike boxing or wrestling clubs, karate schools encourage women to participate.

Unfortunately, karate schools are still scarce in this country. Further, most Americans have no access to the few available schools. Thus, the purpose of this book is to provide the reader with an understanding of basic karate techniques that can be mastered at home. These basic techniques can be learned without extended or intensive practice and are particularly well suited to self-instruction. It is recommended that the reader try to develop a firm command of a few basic karate skills rather than acquire a superficial knowledge of a large variety of moves. In self-defense it is far better to know a few things well than to know many things poorly.

ACKNOWLEDGMENTS

I wish to express my sincere appreciation to my students for their advice and help in preparing this manuscript, but especially I wish to thank Charles Peck for his invaluable help in proofreading the entire manuscript, Linda Lutes and Richard Chin for posing for the photographs, and Bernard MacSweeney for his excellent photography.

CALISTHENICS

Body muscles and joints should be loosened up before participating in any sport. Light exercises designed to loosen the neck, trunk, and legs are recommended for both men and women. However, exercises such as push-ups and sit-ups, although suitable for men, are recommended for women only if their physical strength can bear the strain. The exercises described here do not require special equipment. They can be performed at home, both as part of a daily physical-fitness program and as a preliminary to the practice of self-defense karate. Initially, do the limbering-up calisthenics only for a total of about 15 minutes, repeating each specific exercise about 8 to 12 times. After several days you should find yourself able to increase the time and frequency of each exercise.

NECK EXERCISE

Bend your neck downward as far as possible and then upward.

Turn your head to the left as far as possible and then to the right.

Bend your neck toward your left shoulder and then toward your right shoulder.

BACK-AND-FORTH

SIDE-STRETCHING

Keeping your knees straight, bend down as far as you can.

Stretch backward as far as you can.

Without bending forward, stretch as far as possible to your left side and then to your right.

TWISTING

Keeping your knees straight, bend down and touch your left toes with your right hand, and then do the opposite.

SIT-UPS

Lie on your back with your hands folded behind your head. Keeping your knees straight, sit up, bending forward as far as you can.

PUSH-UPS

Support your weight on your palms and knees.

Lower your body as close to the floor as possible (without actually touching the floor) and then push up to your original position.

A slightly more difficult push-up is performed the same way but with the weight supported on the palms and toes.

LEG STRETCHING

Keeping your right heel flat on the floor, squat down as far as possible with the left leg extended. Repeat on the opposite side.

With the inside of your foot on the floor, stretch your left leg as much as possible. Do the same with the right leg.

LIMBERING-UP KICKS

With the knee of the supporting leg slightly bent, swing the kicking leg upward as far as possible. Do the same with the other leg. This is called the limbering-up front kick.

Starting from the same position as the limbering-up front kick, this time swing your leg upward to the side. Do the same with the other leg. This is the limbering-up side kick.

VITAL SPOTS OF THE HUMAN BODY

Many otherwise well-executed defenses are wasted because the counterattack does not strike a vital spot of the assailant. Consequently, energy is expended uselessly. It is therefore important to know these points of vulnerability and to strike at them in your counterattacks.

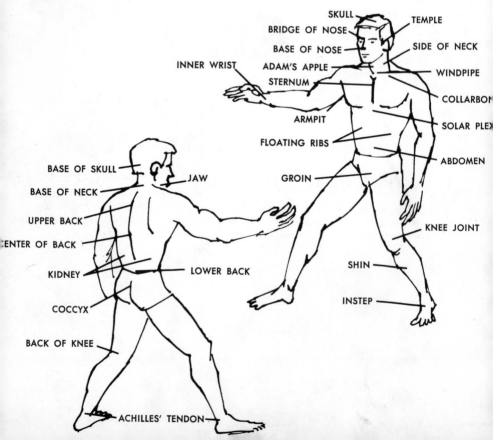

SELF-DEFENSE KARATE

COUNTERATTACKS WHEN
ONE WRIST IS GRABBED

When an assailant attacks, he generally grabs first at the victim's wrist. At this point there are many ways you can defend yourself. As long as the situation permits, you are advised to release the grip (as explained in a later section) and retreat from the situation without injuring the assailant. However, if absolutely necessary, you can counterattack with punches, strikes, and kicks. These can be delivered effectively even by persons who are not karate experts, provided the victim has a good basic knowledge and seizes the opportune moment. Such a counterattack can be particularly effective if the assailant does not expect it.

STRAIGHT FIST PUNCH

The assailant grabs your left hand at the wrist with his right hand.

Extend your left foot slightly forward and clench your right fist at the waist for a fist punch (see page 14, "How To Make a Fist").

Punch the assailant's jaw.

HOW TO MAKE A FIST

First open your hand.

Press the fingertips tightly into your palm and press the thumb over them.

The striking surface is the circled area.

The fist punch is usually delivered from the waist in a thrusting motion. The hand is held palm up, and the arm is close to the body. When the fist has traveled at least half the distance to the target, the wrist twists so that at impact the palm faces down. The striking surface is indicated above. At least two variations of this basic punch are possible. In one, the palm remains up throughout the execution of the punch, and the arm travels in a more distinctly rising arc than the punch described previously. This "uppercut" type of punch is effective at close quarters. In a second variation, the palm faces the body and is used in situations in which the punch originates from a position other than at the waist. The targets for all these punches are the face, chest, ribs, midsection, solar plexus, and groin.

SIDE KICK TO THE MIDSECTION

To execute the side kick, your side must first be facing the target. Bend the supporting knee (the knee farthest from the target), and raise the other leg until the bottom of the foot is opposite the supporting knee. The ankle is flexed and the toes curled upward, as explained below. With a thrusting motion of the hips, propel the leg to the target, striking it with the edge of your foot. After completing the kick, bring your leg back to its starting position and maintain your balance. This kick can be used against the head area, groin, knee, shin, and instep, as well as the midsection.

Again, the assailant grabs your left wrist with his right hand.

After completing the kick, bring your leg to the starting position in order to retain your balance.

Turn your right foot so you are at a right angle to the assailant, simultaneously bending your right knee slightly and raising your left knee.

The striking surface for this kick is the circled area. First curl the toes upward toward the knee and flex the ankle so the outer edge of the foot is toward the target.

In a side thrusting motion, kick to the assailant's midsection.

STAMPING KICK TO THE KNEE

Sometimes an assailant will use both hands to grab the victim's wrist. In this situation a slight variation of the side kick may be used:

The assailant grabs your right wrist with both his hands.

Press the palm of your left hand against his right elbow joint, forcing him to lean far to his left. To facilitate this movement, your right foot should be facing in the same direction, with most of your body weight on your right leg.

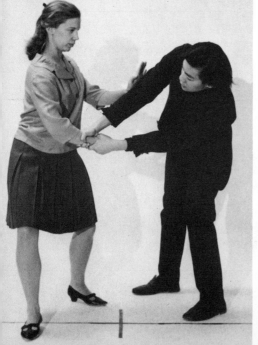

While exerting pressure with your palm, lift your left knee to the side kicking position used previously.

With a side thrusting motion kick his left knee using the edge of your foot. Simultaneously pull your right hand free from his grip.

RELEASE TECHNIQUES

The previous section dealt with counterattacks against an assailant while your wrist is still being held. This section will consider situations in which you release yourself from the grip before counterattacking. The technique for releasing a grip is basically the same for all the situations. In general it can be broken down into the following steps:

- Clench your fist in order to tighten your arm muscles.

- Turn your arm so that you are pulling against his thumb (the weakest part of the gripping hand).

- Bringing your elbow toward your body, release your wrist with a snapping motion of your arm.

THREE EXAMPLES OF RELEASING A GRIP

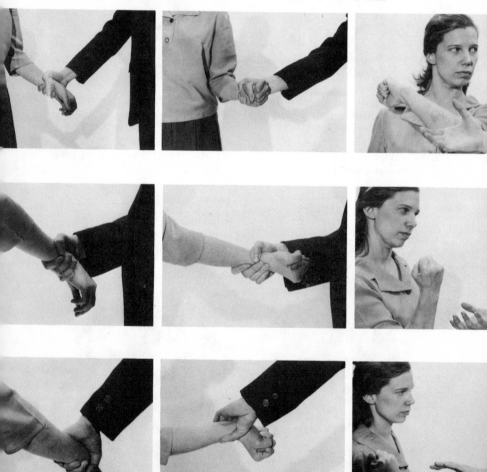

RELEASE AGAINST A ONE-HAND GRIP
FOLLOWED BY A BACK FIST ATTACK

Your left wrist is seized by the assailant's right hand.

Using the method explained previously, free your hand from the grip.

With a snapping motion of your elbow strike the assailant's jaw with the back of your fist. It may be necessary to use other hand and foot attacks also.

The bottom or back fist attack is executed with a snapping motion of the elbow. Initially, the fist is held near your opposite ear as shown in the photograph. The striking surface can be either the bottom or the back of the fist. It should be noted this is a comparatively weak blow, so you should be prepared to follow it up with other attacks. The back fist attack is usually delivered in three different ways: downward, outward, and rising-curve directions.

RELEASE AGAINST A TWO-HAND GRIP
FOLLOWED BY A REVERSE PUNCH

The assailant grabs your left wrist with both hands.

Place your right hand over your own left fist. Tighten your left hand and wrist.

Snap both arms upward toward your body to release the grip. At the same time move your weight to your right leg.

Now shift your body movement back toward the assailant, bringing your elbow toward his face. At the same moment hit his face with the bottom surface of your fist.

You may follow through with your right fist punch.

HAND-TWIST RELEASE

A situation may arise in which you can most easily escape from an assailant's grip by use of a twisting technique. Generally, when applying force in these situations, keep your arm as close to your body as possible, since the farther your arm is extended, the less power it has.

Your right wrist is grabbed by the assailant's left hand.

Pull your arm out and up at the same time.

Step forward on your left foot, going underneath his arm.

Turn around, stepping on your righ[t] foot so that it ends just behind hi[s] left, and raise your left arm, movin[g] his arm up his back.

If he continues to grasp your wris[t] exert further pressure on his arm.

ALTERNATIVE HAND-TWIST RELEASE

Sometimes an alternative of the Hand- twist Release technique can be used, particularly if the assailant begins to pull you.

Your left wrist is grabbed by his left hand and he begins to pull you.

Simply step forward following the direction of the pull and slightly raise your left hand.

Pivot on your left foot, bringing your right foot behind the assailant. Your left arm must always be held close to your body.

Most likely he will release the grip at this point. If not, raise his right hand with both your hands.

You may kick to the back of his knee with the ball of your foot.

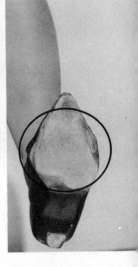

The striking surface for this kick is the circled area.

You can also use an appropriate front kick. In order to execute the front kick, face the target and bend the knee of the supporting leg. Raise the kicking leg so that the knee points toward the target. Pull the lower part of the leg under the thigh as tightly as possible. Curl the toes up and flex the ankle downward. With a snapping motion of the knee, kick the target with the ball of the foot, then immediately bring the leg back to its starting position to maintain your balance. The targets are the same as those for the side kick.

FINGER-TWIST RELEASES

Hurting a finger or a thumb is as effective as hurting the whole arm or body. Since a finger is one of the weakest parts of the body, it is often simpler to release an assailant's grip by twisting a finger or thumb. This kind of move is particularly effective when you cannot resist the assailant by matching your strength against his. Such a finger-twisting attack may be applied not only when your wrist is grabbed, but also whenever your hand is free to execute the twist.

THUMB TWIST FOLLOWED BY A
FRONT KICK TO THE KNEE

Assailant grabs you by the wrist.

Place your free thumb against the inner surface of his thumb.

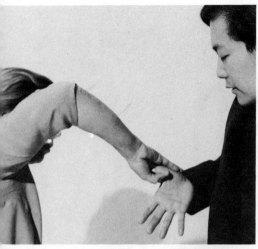

With your thumb, exert pressure toward his wrist in an upward direction. Pressing it with a snapping motion will usually cause the assailant to release the grip.

Raise your knee if it is necessary to deliver a kick.

Kick to his knee or to his groin or shin.

TWISTING A FINGER

Your left wrist is grabbed by the assailant's right hand.

Raise your left hand so that the assailant's hand is palm up. Move your body slightly toward him. The raising motion may weaken the grip.

Press his little finger with your free thumb in an outward and downward direction. The finger twist begins in a snapping motion.

Press the finger strongly and continuously. You may twist other fingers if you find them more convenient. Then you may continue to attack by using any convenient kick or punch.

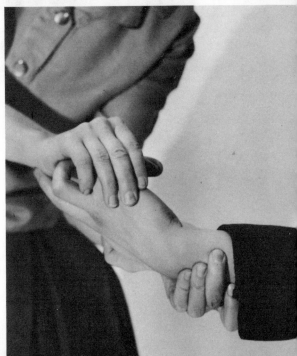

COUNTERATTACKS WHEN BOTH WRISTS ARE GRABBED

Assailants seldom attack a person by grabbing both wrists. However, the situation might conceivably arise, and you should know and practice some defenses against this kind of attack. In general, three different defenses can be used: release only one hand and use it for a counterattack; release both hands and follow up with a counterattack; or kick the assailant without first releasing the grip. You do not always need to have your hands free from a grip in order to deliver a successful kick. Kicking techniques are obviously advantageous in any situation in which both hands are held.

KNEE KICK

Both wrists are grabbed.

Move toward the assailant, spreading your arms outward.

Deliver a knee kick to his groin. The thrust of the kick comes from raising your hip. Such a kick is usually made to a target that is at close range.

Striking surface for knee kick.

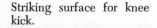

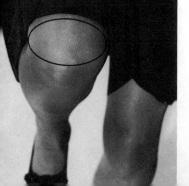

In the knee kick the leg is held in exactly the same way as for the front kick. However, the power comes from a thrusting motion of the hips, instead of the snapping motion of the knee as in the front kick. The targets are mainly face and groin.

KNIFE-HAND STRIKE
(PRECEDED BY FREEING ONE HAND)

Both wrists are grabbed.

Rotate your body slightly so that you face the assailant sideways.

Release just your left hand. Note that while pulling your left hand with a snapping motion to release it from the grip, your entire body leans away from the assailant.

Deliver a knife-hand strike with the freed hand to assailant's neck. Your upper body moves back toward him as you strike.

Make a knife-hand by opening your hand wide and tensing your hand muscles. The first and second joints of the fingers are slightly bent, but the bottom joint stays unbent. Tighten all the fingers together and force them backward, while tucking the thumb down. Make an outward knife-hand strike by striking with the outer surface of the hand. Bring the striking hand over the opposite side shoulder, and then deliver the strike by snapping the hand out to the target in a forward and outward arc. The targets are head, face, neck, ribs, and body joints.

DOUBLE-FIST PUNCH TO THE CHIN
(PRECEDED BY FREEING BOTH HANDS)

In a snapping motion, pull both your hands inward and backward against his thumb, at the same time shifting your body weight backward and sitting down slightly on your rear leg.

Both wrists are grabbed.

Step slightly toward assailant while spreading both hands to the sides.

Shift your body weight forward toward the assailant and punch his chin with both hands. You may add kicking techniques if necessary.

HAND-TWIST RELEASE

Both wrists are grabbed.

Grab assailant's right wrist with your right hand. Step slightly forward with your left foot.

While slightly lowering yourself, pivot around to your right underneath his arms, at the same time raising them a short distance.

At this point the assailant should be fairly well incapacitated; however, follow up with additional attacks if necessary.

Position of hands in the release shown above.

COUNTERATTACKS WHEN HELD AROUND THE BODY FROM THE FRONT

Sometimes, rather than grabbing for an arm or wrist, an assailant may attack by encircling the waist or chest. Releasing yourself from such a hold is relatively simple. Since your arms are not held your hands are free to attack the assailant. The assailant is at a further disadvantage since his hands are occupied holding you. Using the knuckles, elbows, fingertips, and palm-heel, you can strike at vital spots on the face and neck. Also various kicking techniques aimed at the foot, shin, knee, and groin can be used effectively. These moves are particularly recommended for women because they can be applied successfully without requiring a great deal of preliminary practice. Following such moves, additional punches, strikes, or kicks can be used to incapacitate the assailant.

PALM-HEEL THRUST (TO NOSE) AND
PALM-HEEL ATTACK (TO JAW)

Assailant grasps victim about the waist.

Use your left palm to thrust against his nose. Your body tilts slightly toward the right in order to provide thrusting force.

If he still holds you, raise your right hand.

Then deliver a palm-heel attack, executed in a forward and inward direction, striking his jaw with the palm-heel.

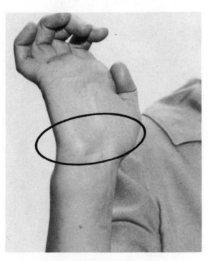

Striking surface for the palm-heel attack.

A palm-heel is made simply by opening your hand wide and tight, and pressing the hand backward. The palm-heel attack is usually made in forward, upward, downward, and hooking directions. The hooking attack that was applied in the above situation is performed by thrusting the palm forward and inward in an arc and hooking it at impact. You may attack any vital spots on the face with the palm-heel.

PALM-HEEL ATTACK (TO TEMPLE) WITH BOTH HANDS

Again, assailant grabs you about the waist.

If the assailant holds you tightly, raise both your hands.

Using both hands simultaneously, deliver palm-heel attacks to his temples. You can also grab his ears and pull his head back.

Kick his shin with the toe of your shoe or stamp at his instep.

DEFENSE WITH CHOKING ATTACK

Again, assailant grabs you about the waist.

Release his hold by choking him with your hands. Push his chin away with your left hand and at the same time grab his windpipe with your right hand and squeeze. This pressure should force him to release his hold in order to keep from choking.

KNUCKLE ATTACKS

If the assailant's hold is too tight for you to move, you can make enough distance for a right-hand knuckle attack by first pushing his neck with your left hand. Then use one of the following knuckle attacks.

To the throat (also nose and eyes)   Striking surface

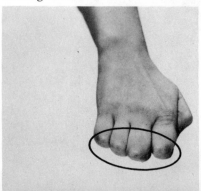

To the eyes (also base and bridge of nose)   Striking surface

To the temple (also side of neck)   Striking surface

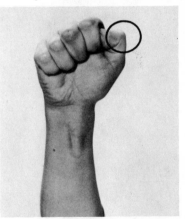

To the eyes (also throat)   Striking surface

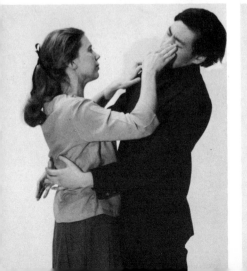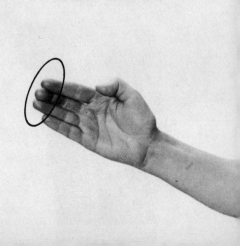

WHEN BOTH HANDS ARE TRAPPED

When an assailant grabs you about the waist or chest, your arms may not be free to attack. When your hands are trapped and your body is tightly held, you cannot hope to escape with a simple kick or a hand technique. First force the assailant to loosen his hold temporarily. To accomplish this, use any sudden or shocking move such as a forehead strike, scratching, stamping on his foot, or kicking his shin. Afterward you can follow through with a strong move.

Assailant grabs you around the waist, trapping both arms.

Hit his chin or nose with your forehead. All you can expect from this attack is a shocking impact to weaken his hold temporarily.

Immediately raise both arms and at the same time lower your body to escape from his hold.

Escape by shifting backward.

Employ a knee kick to his groin, or, as an alternative, a front kick.

In addition you may add an inward elbow attack to his face.

COUNTERATTACKS WHEN
HELD FROM THE REAR

When you are seized from the rear, use whatever moves you can that have a shocking impact in order to free yourself from the grip. Attacks with the back of the head to the assailant's face, a stamping kick to his instep or shin, or a finger twist are some of the preliminary moves that may be applied in such situations. Then, follow through with strong hand and foot techniques.

While walking, you are attacked and your clothing is grabbed from the rear.

Step forward on your left foot bringing your left arm across your body. Lower yourself slightly for balance by bending your knees and hips.

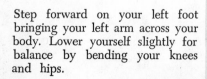

Strike into the assailant's midsection with your left elbow. Note that as you attack your body twists toward him for thrusting power.

Snap your left hand into his face, striking with the back of your fist.

WITH YOUR ARMS FREE

Assailant grabs you around the waist, leaving your arms free.

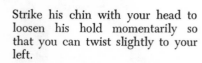

Strike his chin with your head to loosen his hold momentarily so that you can twist slightly to your left.

Attack his eyes with the fingertips of your left hand.

Thrust your left elbow backward into his midsection while lowering your body and twisting it to the left.

WITH YOUR ARMS TRAPPED

Assailant grabs you around the waist, trapping your arms.

Raise your left knee.

Stamp on his instep (or kick his shin with your heel).

To release his hold, raise your arms, simultaneously stepping to the side with both feet and lowering your hips into a sitting position.

Strike his midsection with your left elbow.

Strike his face with the back of your left fist.

COUNTERATTACKS
WHEN BEING CHOKED

Choking attacks constitute a deadly threat. You must immediately do everything possible to save yourself. First lower your chin to tighten your neck muscles, simultaneously using your hands to weaken the choke. If you have room to move back, always try to move your body away from the assailant's hands either during or following your counterattacks.

RELEASING A FRONT CHOKE
AND COUNTERATTACKING

Assailant chokes you from the front.

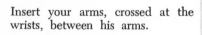

Insert your arms, crossed at the wrists, between his arms.

Break the choke by pressing with your arms outward and forward against his, and at the same time shift backward to get away from the choke.

Attack him with a knee kick to the groin. (Seizing his lapels enables you to pull him into the kick for more thrusting power.)

ALTERNATE DEFENSE AGAINST FRONT CHOKE

Assailant chokes you from the front.

Stepping back slightly on your right foot, strike his left arm with your left arm, simultaneously raising your right arm.

Stepping back and shifting your weight to your left leg, strike the outside of his left arm with your right arm. Note that you now face him on the side.

Twisting your hips, shift your weight to your right leg and punch to his midsection with your left hand.

PALM-HEEL THRUST WHILE
BEING CHOKED AGAINST A WALL

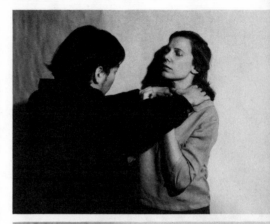

You are held against a wall and you cannot move backward.

Hit his chin with the heel of your left palm.

At the same time, kick into his groin with your left knee.

PRESSING ASSAILANT'S ELBOWS
WHEN BEING CHOKED AGAINST WALL

Raise your arms outside of his with your palms open.

Strike his elbows with your palms, and in a simultaneous inward, upward, and forward direction, push him back.

Kick into his groin with your left foot *and*

Use an uppercut punch to strike his chin, if another attack is necessary.

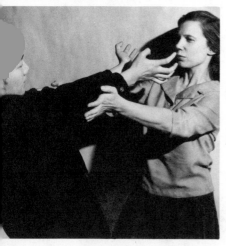

FINGERTIP ATTACK WHEN BEING CHOKED ON THE FLOOR

With the fingertips of the same hand attack his eyes immediately.

When the assailant straddles you and begins to choke you, raise your closed fists between his arms to loosen his hands, releasing some of the pressure of the choke.

Strike his chin with the heel of your palm.

Punch to the side of his neck with your other hand.

If necessary, seize his Adam's apple between your thumb and fingers.

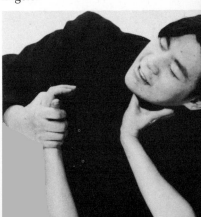

DEFENSE FROM A REAR CHOKE

Assailant chokes you from the rear.

Attack his eyes with your left fingertips. At the same time, seize his right wrist with your right hand to release the pressure of the choke.

Pulling down on his wrist, bend forward and attack his groin with your left hand, using the bottom of your fist.

Move your head from under his arm, keeping your hold on his wrist. At the same time twist around to the left, placing your left foot behind his right.

Raise his arm with both of your hands toward the middle of his back. If he continues to struggle, increase pressure on his arm.

DEFENSE WHEN
ATTACKED WHILE SITTING DOWN

It is possible that you might be attacked while sitting down, for example, at a movie theater or on a park bench. Such an attack may be either a deadly threat or a mere annoyance. In the case of a deadly attack, you must immediately respond with counterattacks. You can counterattack from a sitting position or you may first stand up and then counterattack. In the case of less serious attacks, often you need only use sufficient force to discourage the molester from continuing. Should he then respond with a deadly attack, you may counterattack appropriately.

WHEN THE ASSAILANT PUTS
HIS HAND ON YOUR KNEE

A man sitting next to you places his right hand on your left knee and intends to molest you.

Place your right hand over his.

Standing up, use both hands to press against his wrist joint by twisting it around inward and upward.

If absolutely necessary, you can continue by executing a front kick to his neck or face with your right foot, while keeping your hold on his right hand.

WHEN THE ASSAILANT PUTS HIS ARM AROUND YOUR SHOULDERS

A man sitting next to you puts his left hand on your left knee and his right arm around your shoulders, intending to molest you.

Place your left arm under his right so that your forearm is at a right angle to his arm, between his elbow and shoulder.

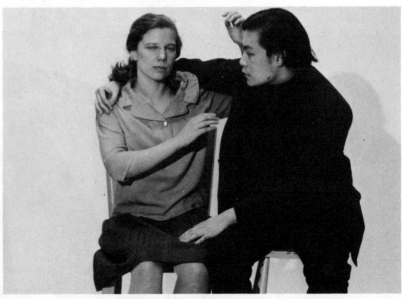

Join your hands together, stand up, and simultaneously press against his elbow while shifting your weight to your right.

DEFENSE FROM THE FLOOR

If attacked it is possible that you might fall down, as the result of a blow, of being pushed or tripped, or simply from losing your balance. However, you can still defend yourself from the ground by using kicks. To kick effectively from a lying-down position you must first pull your body compactly together. A kick from a spread-out position will never stop an assailant.

From a lying-down position, you may bring your knee toward your chest and, when the assailant comes toward you, kick with the outer edge of your foot to . . .

his knee

his midsection

his face

Or, you may bend your knee back and kick with the ball of your foot in a circular motion (roundhouse kick) to . . .

his groin

his face

DEFENSE AGAINST WEAPONS

Attacks with weapons are the most dangerous type of assault. Generally, if an assailant is armed it is best not to resist. In the case of a knife, run if you can. In the case of a gun, follow the assailant's instructions. However, if there is no alternative there are defensive moves you can make.

OVERHEAD ATTACK WITH A KNIFE

Assailant threatens you with a raised knife.

Stepping to the right, strike his arm with your left arm.

Shifting your weight to your left foot, attack his chin with an uppercut punch.

STRAIGHT THRUST ATTACK WITH A KNIFE

Assailant threatens you with knife at waist level.

Step back with your right foot, simultaneously rotate your body to your right so that your side faces him. At the same time thrust his arm aside with your left hand and seize his hand with your right.

Twist his hand around a[n]
bend it upward against h[is]
wrist.

Deliver a front kick into his
midsection with your right
leg.

PISTOL ATTACK

A pistol is pointed at you from the front.

With your left hand, push his right hand inward while tilting your body to the left. Step forward and to the side with your left foot, and simultaneously grasp the pistol barrel with your right hand.

Press the pistol barrel upward against the wrist.

Kick into his groin with your right foot.